DOES MY LIFE MATTER?

Written By Dr. Tamecca S. Rogers and Keith Ross

Illustrate by: Arushan Art

About the Authors

Dr. Tamecca Rogers holds a bachelor's degree in psychology, a master's in business administration, and a doctoral degree in educational leadership. Dr. Rogers served five years as a hospital corpsman in the United States Navy and a combined six years as a high school instructor and college enrollment counselor. She has also held adjunct professor positions at multiple postsecondary institutions. Dr. Rogers has worked at Tulsa Technology Center since 2010 and currently holds the position of the Director of Diversity, Equity, and Inclusion. She is the proud mom of Ian, Chazen, and Keith, and lives in Tulsa, Oklahoma with her family.

Keith Ross is a fourth grader who loves video games, Beyblades, road trips, modeling, and acting. Keith has his own unique style and dances to his own beat. He lives in Tulsa, Oklahoma with his family.

Keith has co-authored Now You're It: Journaling to Perseverance, Momma May I Be Me?, Daddy May I Decide?, and A Promise Deferred: The Massacre of Black Wall Street, with his mother, Dr. Rogers, and this is his fifth book.

ISBN Number: 978-1-7365426-2-0
Library of Congress Control Number: 2021901143

Published by Inspire Publishing LLC
P.O. Box 691608
Tulsa, OK 74169-1608, USA

Inspire Publishing LLC

Dedication

I dedicate this book to my three sons: Ian, Chazen, and Keith. May they become resilient and unwavering Black men, while shining in the glory and rich history of their ancestors. —Tamecca Rogers

I dedicate this book to my friends and teachers. — Keith Ross

I'll never forget the day at school when my best friend Max invited me to his birthday party.

He was turning seven years old and boy was he excited.

"Keith, my mom said she will invite Captain Legit to my party," he told me with a beaming smile.

Captain Legit was our favorite comic book superhero. We both loved Captain Legit. In fact, most kids did because Captain Legit fought for justice for everyone. He was cool.

"Wow, that is awesome, Max," I said.

And it really was. I was super excited to be going to my best friend's party and to see my favorite superhero. I couldn't wait.

Maybe Captain Legit could even teach us a few of his moves, I thought.

When I arrived home from school that day, my mom could tell I was excited about something.

"Someone had an amazing day at school," she said with a happy chuckle.

"My day was more than amazing," I said. "It was super fantastic, especially since I got invited to Max's birthday party on Saturday. Can I go, Mom, please?"

"Well, that is fantastic! And I don't see why you can't go. Just make sure your chores are done and your room is clean," she said. "What present do you plan to get him?"

"Something to do with Captain Legit. That's our favorite superhero," I said.

"Excellent," Mom said. "Maybe we can pick something up for him Friday after school."

"Yayyy!" I jumped with joy.

After I finished my homework, Mom called me downstairs for dinner. Dad had finally made it home from work.

So, we sat down to eat together as we normally did, but something was bothering Dad.

I could tell he didn't want to say anything while I was around because he didn't want me to worry. He is caring like that.

After dinner, I overheard Dad tell Mom an older white lady called the police on him when he was walking back to work with a cup of coffee.

"She told the cops I looked suspicious because there have been a few break-ins in that part of town," he whispered to Mom.

When it was time for bed, Mom read me a story and tucked me in.

Before she left my room, I asked her why the older white lady thought Dad looked suspicious.

I didn't understand because Dad always wears a suit to work and nothing ever looks suspicious about him.

Mom sighed and said, "Well, sweetie, not everyone in America is treated the same. And because your father was the only Black man in the area, the lady assumed he was the one committing the crimes. Sometimes we get blamed for things we didn't do, just because of the color of our skin."

I became sad. Not my dad. He is a great guy and has a big heart. "That's why the Black Lives Matter Movement exists," Mom continued to explain. "As Black people, we are sometimes treated unfairly, so we must work extra hard to change things and make it known our lives matter, too."

I had seen people with Black Lives Matter signs, but now I understand more of what they stand for.

"White people sometimes don't understand the struggles we face just in being Black. The Black Lives Matter Movement is a good way to point out injustices and inequality to them. You might be able to help your friends at school see that. They're good kids, but they might not know what it's like being a Black person," Mom said before I went to sleep.

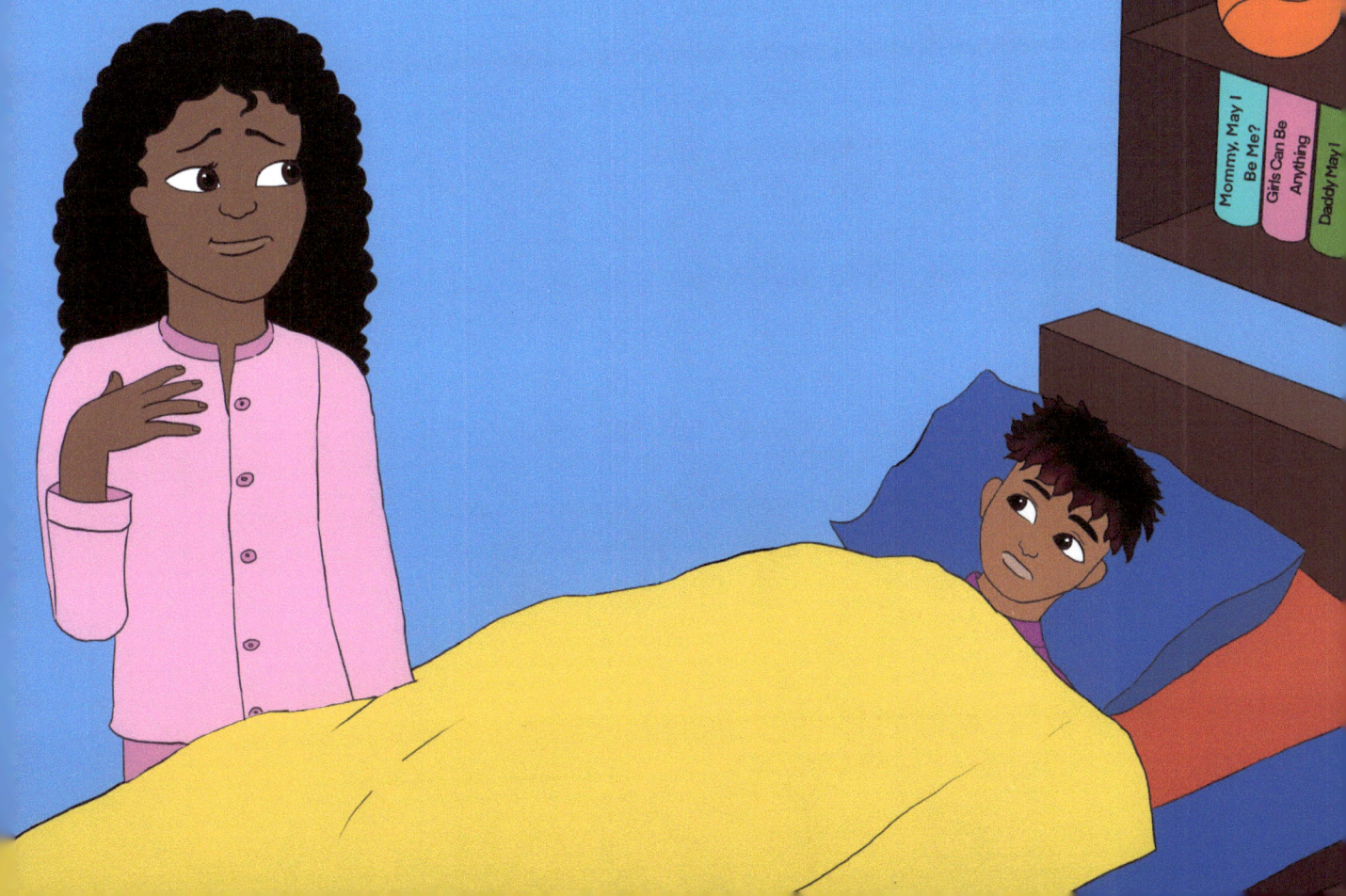

The next day at school, my teacher Mrs. Karalson gave us an interesting assignment to write a letter to the government telling them Black Lives Matter and new laws should be created to protect Black people.

She told us, "Black Lives Matter is a social movement that formed to protest against incidents of police brutality and any racially motivated violence against Black people. Do you remember the death of George Floyd?"

We all nodded.

"Well, that's an example of police brutality." She then described some of the suspicion and mistreatment Black people experienced simply for the color of their skin.

I immediately thought about my dad the night before. Max raised his hand and asked, "But shouldn't we write a letter saying All Lives Matter instead? Surely, everyone is important, not just Black people?"

It shocked me Max didn't realize the significance of the difference. It was sad because he was my best friend.

Other classmates who were also invited to Max's birthday party agreed with Max.

"Well, Max, you bring up a great point," Mrs. Karalson said with enthusiasm. "But Black Lives Matter does not mean only Black Lives Matter. It just means we are focusing on creating equality for everyone since cops don't target other races as much."

I looked back at Max and could see from his face he didn't understand. My other white friends also looked confused.

At lunch, I sat with Max and some of our friends. All he could talk about was his birthday party.

But I felt I needed to bring up the Black Lives Matter conversation from class.

"So, how do you feel about the letter assignment?"
I asked everyone.

"Well, I just don't believe in Black Lives Matter because I believe in
All Lives Matter," Max said.

Everyone at the table nodded.

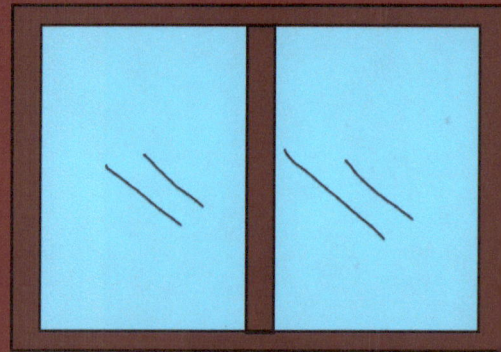

"But when you say you don't believe in Black Lives Matter, you are saying you don't believe my life matters," I said with frustration.

"No, I believe your life matters and my life, too," Max said. "That's why All Lives Matter!"

I tried to repeat what the teacher said, but it was difficult to get Max or anyone else to understand, and this saddened me.

At home that evening, Mom saw I was frowning.

"What's the matter, baby boy?" she asked.

"Max doesn't understand why Black Lives Matter and not All Lives," I said.

Mom rubbed my head, and I eventually rested it on her shoulder.

"Max is a good kid and you're his best friend. You just have to find a creative way to explain to him why Black Lives Matter is important. Then I think he will listen and understand," Mom said.

The rest of that evening, I thought long and hard about how to help Max and the other kids understand.

I thought so hard my head hurt, so I took a break and read a Captain Legit comic instead.

After reading the comic, the answer hit me.
It was perfect. I went to bed feeling relaxed,
I know exactly what I will say to my friends
tomorrow.

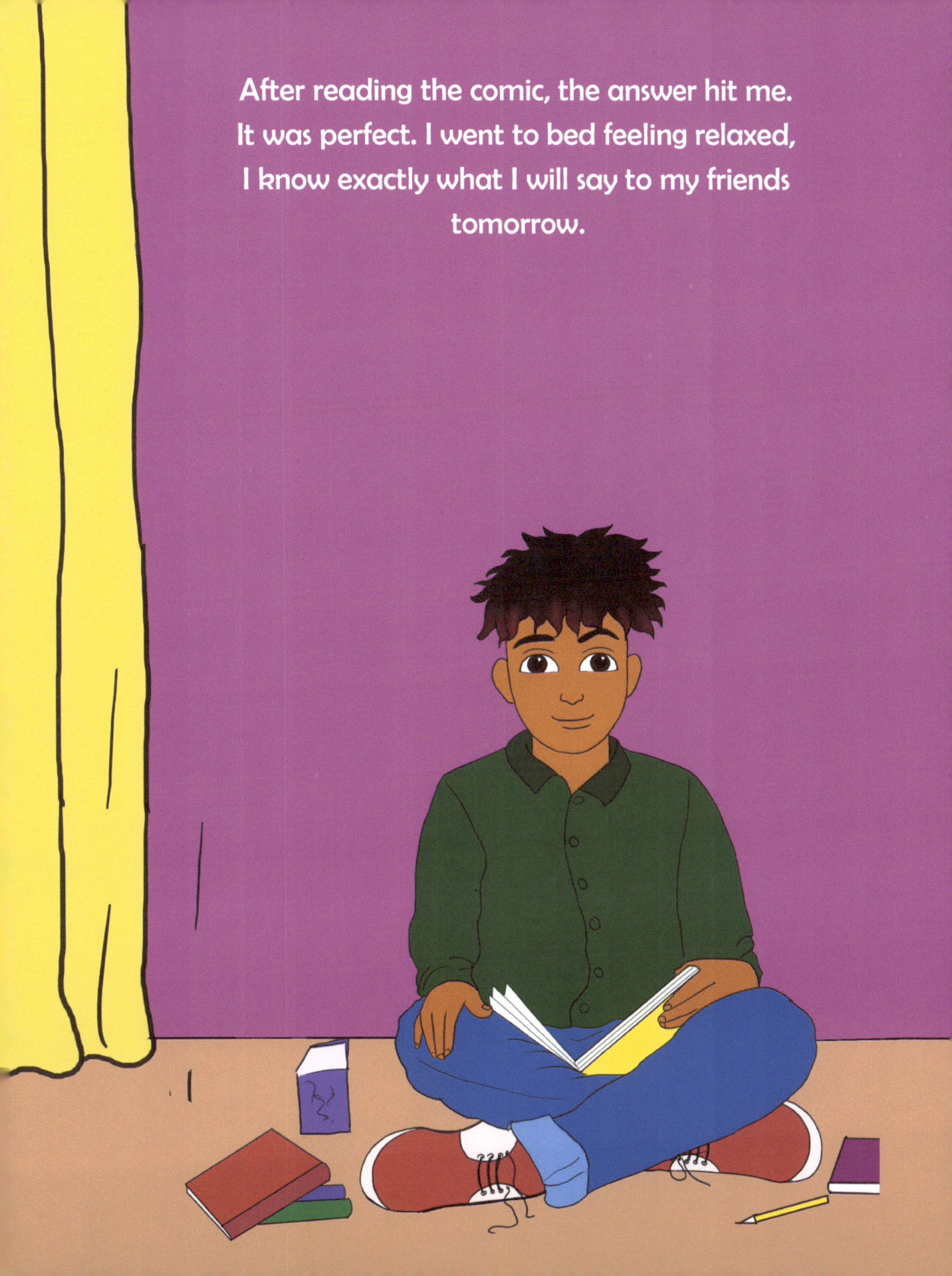

The day of Max's birthday finally came.

He was very excited, especially when his mom brought out the Captain Legit themed cake. After we sang happy birthday, Captain Legit himself appeared!

Max's parents served cake and ice cream, while Max got a photo with Captain Legit.

Eventually, every kid there, including myself, also got a photo with him. I was so happy to pose with my superhero.

Finally, it was time for Max to open his gifts. One of them was a football. He also got a new video game. And finally, he opened my gift.

It was the newest Captain Legit comic. I could tell by the look on his face it was his favorite gift.

After he finished opening his gifts, Max and some of our other friends began to play tag.

When we were all tired, I felt it was the perfect time to explain to them about Black Lives Matter.

"So, does everyone agree Captain Legit is our favorite hero?" I asked.

"Yes," they all said in unison.

"And Captain Legit has saved people in burning buildings and stopped villains from destroying his city, correct?"
"Yes," everyone said again.

"Well, what if someone asked Captain Legit why he didn't pay attention to the other buildings when he stopped the burning one, or why he didn't go off to save other cities when he saved his own?" I asked.

"Well, that's just silly," Max said. "The other buildings are not burning, and the other cities are not as violent as his city. That doesn't mean the other buildings are less important, though."

"Exactly," I said. "That's the same as the Black Lives Matter movement."

Max and our other friends stopped and thought about that for a moment.

"Wow, I never thought of it like that," Max said.
"Yeah, me neither," another friend added.

When everyone finally understood, they apologized to me by giving me a big hug. They said they would be an ally to the Black Lives Matter movement and enjoy writing their letter.

My mom had arrived, and she heard what they said and saw the love and support my friends gave me.

She winked at me and I winked back happily. Captain Legit had come to the rescue yet again, this time on an issue very important to me.

www.ingramcontent.com/pod-product-compliance
Lightning Source LLC
Chambersburg PA
CBHW060811270326
41928CB00003B/59